Cheerleading

Ellen Rusconi

Children's Press
A Division of Scholastic Inc.
New York / Toronto / London / Auckland / Sydney
Mexico City / New Delhi / Hong Kong
Danbury, Connecticut

Special thanks to Northern Virginia Tigers

To Delilah and all of her cheerleaders

Book Design: Michelle Innes
Contributing Editor: Eric Fein

Photo Credits: Cover, p. 1 © Maura Boruchow; p. 5 © AP Worldwide Photos; p. 6 © ClassMates.com Yearbook Archive; p. 9 © Imagebank; pp. 10, 12, 15, 17-18, 20, 23-24, 26-32, 34-36, 38 © Maura Boruchow; p. 40 © AP Worldwide Photos

Visit Children's Press on the Internet at:
http://publishing.grolier.com

Library of Congress Cataloging-in-Publication Data

Rusconi, Ellen.
   Cheerleading / Ellen Rusconi.
     p. cm. -- (After school)
   Includes bibliographical references and index.
   ISBN 0-516-23148-0 (lib. bdg.) -- ISBN 0-516-29552-7 (pbk.)
   1. Cheerleading--Juvenile literature. [1. Cheerleading.] I. Title. II. Series

LB3635 .R87 2001
791.6'4--dc21

                       00-065725

CONTENTS

INTRODUCTION

Do you like to dance, tumble, and jump? Do you want to show spirit for your school? Do you enjoy performing in front of people? If you answered "yes" to any of these questions, cheerleading may be perfect for you!

Cheerleading is a unique sport. It combines athletics with enthusiasm and leadership. The best cheerleaders jump high, dance, and tumble. At the same time, they are able to yell and cheer. Cheerleading plays an important role in sports—whether it is for a school or a pro team.

Cheerleading is a good way to develop a positive attitude. It gives you a chance to socialize and make friends. Though cheerleading is hard work, it also is a lot of fun!

This book will introduce you to the world of cheerleading. You will learn some of the basic cheer routines. You will learn how to motivate a crowd. You'll also get helpful hints for doing well at cheerleading tryouts.

Cheerleading is a popular part of most sporting events. These women are cheerleaders for the St. Louis Rams football team.

Cameron Diaz

Madonna

Sandra Bullock

Sandra Bullock, Cameron Diaz, and Madonna
were all cheerleaders in high school.

CHAPTER ONE

Getting Started

If you dream of being a cheerleader, you're in good company. Cheerleading provides the chance to perform for an audience. It's not surprising that many celebrities were once cheerleaders. Christina Aguilera, Sandra Bullock, Cameron Diaz, and Madonna were all cheerleaders. Luke Perry was the mascot at his high school. Even President George W. Bush participated in college cheerleading.

Did You Know?

Eighty-three percent of student cheerleaders in the United States are leaders in student organizations. Eighty-three percent of student cheerleaders have a B average or above in school.

HISTORY

When most people think of cheerleading, they picture teenagers in school outfits cheering for their teams. The history of cheerleading is more interesting than that. In fact, cheerleading didn't start in the United States. It began way back in the year 776 B.C., in ancient Greece. During the first Olympic games, people cheered for their favorite runners.

In the United States, organized cheerleading began in 1898 at the University of Minnesota. Johnny Campbell, a medical student, decided to test the idea that crowd support might help a team on to victory. He had six male students lead the crowd in cheers. Campbell called them the Yell Captains. His idea worked. The cheering made the football games more fun for both the athletes and the fans.

All cheerleaders were males until the 1920s. That was when cheerleaders began to add stunts and gymnastics to their routines. Because women were easier to lift than men, women were welcomed onto cheerleading squads.

During World War II (1939–1945), young men were drafted for military service. So cheerleading squads became mostly female. Women have dominated the sport ever since. It is important to note that the best squads today have both men and women cheerleaders. The increased demand

Only men were cheerleaders when cheerleading began in the United States.

Yell Captain

9

Women became cheerleaders in the 1920s. Today, women dominate the sport.

of athletics—with more lifts, throws, and gymnastics—have made men valuable to squads that compete.

WHAT IT TAKES TO BE A CHEERLEADER

American cheerleading has come a long way since its early days in Minnesota. Today, cheerleading is a demanding, competitive sport.

In fact, some people believe that it may become a future Olympic sport. Anyone who has cheered for an entire game knows how hard that is. Cheerleading is as physically challenging as the sports it supports.

Physical Conditioning

As with all sports, cheerleading requires conditioning to prevent injury. You should always warm up and stretch before cheerleading. Warming up eases your muscles into your workout instead of shocking them with sudden motion. There are several ways to warm up. You

Did You Know?

There are more than three million cheerleaders in the United States! About eight out of ten of these cheerleaders are ages 14–18.

It is important to warm up and stretch before beginning cheerleading routines.

might jog, do low-impact aerobics, or just move around. Any of these activities will increase the blood flow to your muscles and loosen them up. Warming up should be followed by stretching.

Stretching promotes flexibility and reduces muscle strain. To get in shape for cheerleading,

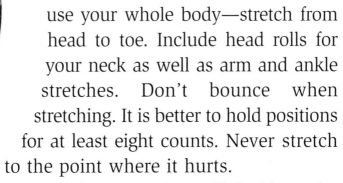

use your whole body—stretch from head to toe. Include head rolls for your neck as well as arm and ankle stretches. Don't bounce when stretching. It is better to hold positions for at least eight counts. Never stretch to the point where it hurts.

You and your coaches will decide on the kind of conditioning that's right for you. Abdominal crunches, push-ups, weight training, and other kinds of strength conditioning are great for cheerleaders. A stronger body means steadier lifts, higher jumps, and increased endurance. Being flexible also is important for performing splits and jumps.

When warming up and conditioning, don't forget to train your voice as well. Breathe deeply and yell from your chest, not your throat. You'll be louder if you practice cheering in a low pitch rather than in a high, shrill voice.

Cheerleading Gear

As cheerleading has become more athletic, so have cheerleading uniforms. In the 1950s, cheerleaders wore long skirts and sweaters. That would be unthinkable today. No one can jump, dance, and tumble comfortably in a long skirt.

On game days, cheerleaders usually wear uniforms. Women wear shirts, vests, or sweaters and short skirts with shorts. Men wear shirts or sweaters and close-fitting shorts or pants.

Why do cheerleaders wear tight outfits? Jumps and movements look better when the lines of the body can be seen clearly. To prevent injury, a cheerleader's body needs to be well defined. The members of the squad who are spotting the cheerleaders will be able to catch them safely in case of a fall. When practicing, cheerleaders should keep this in mind. Fitted shorts along with workout pants and tops are best for practice.

Cheerleaders wear team
uniforms. Women wear
shirts and skirts. Men
wear shirts and pants.

15

Good shoes are very important for cheerleaders. Cheering at a game means being on your feet for at least two hours. You need comfortable, well-cushioned shoes that are both flexible and supportive. They should be flexible for dance moves and well-cushioned and supportive for jumps. Most squad members wear sneakers or athletic shoes. Some squads require all cheerleaders to wear the same shoes as part of

Did You Know?

Pom-poms (also known as pom-pons or poms) usually were made of paper. They were delivered to the squads flat. Then the cheerleaders crinkled the poms a few strands at a time. It took a few hours to make them full!

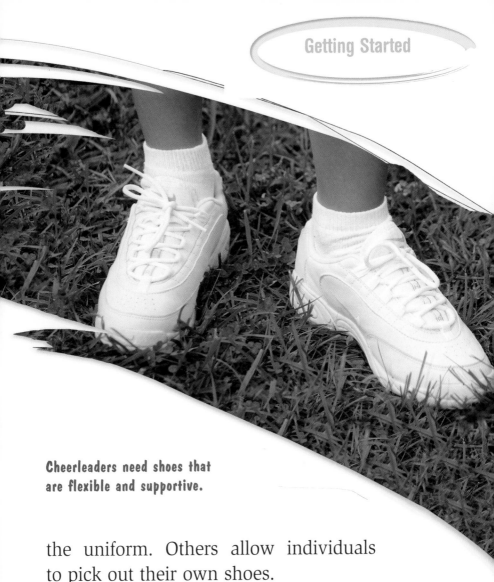

Cheerleaders need shoes that
are flexible and supportive.

the uniform. Others allow individuals
to pick out their own shoes.

   Cheerleading squads add additional gear to
suit their styles. Anything that raises spirit and
enthusiasm is welcome. Megaphones and pom-
poms are most commonly used to rally the fans.

CHAPTER TWO

Joining a Squad

Cheerleading tryouts can make people nervous. Here are a few simple guidelines you can follow to take the pressure off.

Types of Teams

Find out what types of cheerleading squads you can join in your community. Most junior high and high schools have cheerleading squads. Many towns have squads that perform dance routines to music. These groups include dance teams, majorettes, color guards, and pom-pom squads. Majorettes twirl batons. Color guards perform with banners and flags. Pom-pom squads use pom-poms in their routines. If you prefer the dancing part of cheerleading, one of these squads may be right for you. If you're interested in leading

Most junior high and high schools have cheerleading squads.

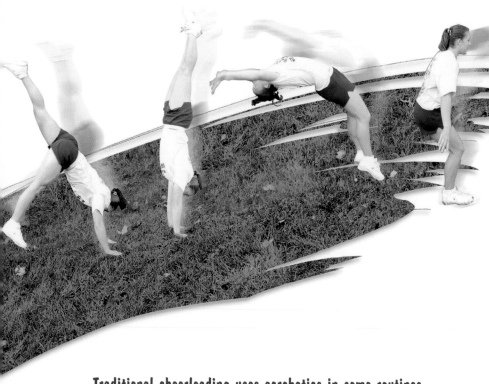

Traditional cheerleading uses acrobatics in some routines.

cheers, then try a pep squad. If you want to combine these skills with acrobatics and jumps, then try traditional cheerleading.

Cheerleading teams are active in a variety of sports in most towns. Many football, hockey, wrestling, and basketball teams have cheerleading squads. Decide which sport you'd like to cheer for, and then go for it.

Preparing for Tryouts

Some squads hold tryouts at the very end of a sports season for the next year. Others do it at the beginning of a season. Find out who coaches the squad and when tryouts take place. Ask the coach what he or she looks for at tryouts. Will you need to do jumps or a split? This way, you can practice ahead of time. Many people want to be cheerleaders, but they are afraid to try out. Knowing what to expect can make tryouts go more smoothly.

Most squads hold a practice week before tryouts to teach everyone chants, cheers, and certain skills. Chants are short cheers performed on the sidelines. They have limited movement and are done while the game is going on. Cheers are longer routines, often with jumps or stunts. Cheers are performed during time-outs or between game periods. You will be taught some of the basic cheers, chants, and jumps during practice week. The people teaching you will be the coaches and the returning squad members. Your tryout will take place before a panel of judges.

Everyone trying out for the first time is on equal footing. During practice week, make sure you dress neatly and arrive on time. Pay attention and work hard. Coaches and captains expect dedication and effort. They need to see that you are serious about cheerleading. They want to feel that you will continue to work hard if you make the team. The more often you practice cheers, the better prepared you will be on tryout day.

Tryouts

Being confident will improve your chances of making the team. It can be hard to perform cheers in front of judges. But if you make the squad, you will be performing in front of large crowds. The judges want to see you perform with poise.

The coach helps beginning cheerleaders learn the basic moves and review the cheers.

There are some simple things you can do to help you have a good tryout. Make sure you've practiced your routines. Wear simple clothes that fit well and are not too tight or too loose. Pull your hair back and away from your eyes. If you have questions, ask them. The coaches will be happy to help you. If you make a mistake, don't panic. Continue with your cheer until it is done.

24

CHAPTER THREE

Essential Skills and Movements

All cheerleading squads have their own routines. However, some common moves are used throughout the country. Mastering these basic movements will help you learn cheers more quickly and easily.

MOTION AND TECHNIQUE

There are some basic rules to remember in performing motions used in cheers and chants. Each position should be sharp and clean. Movements shouldn't flow from one to the other. Instead, you should feel as if you hit each position. Then move quickly to the next position. Keep your wrists rigid and your hand movements precise. Extend or stretch each position. If every member of the squad does this, cheers and chants will look uniform and synchronized.

Knowing the basic movements makes it easier to perform all kinds of cheerleading routines.

HAND, ARM, AND LEG MOTIONS

Most cheers are made up of a few basic hand, arm, and leg positions. Once you master them, you can learn cheers more quickly. You also can create your own cheers and chants by combining different movements. Here are some basic positions.

hands

Hands straight out, flat from the wrists, with fingers pressed together

Blades

Hands in fists with thumbs outside of fingers, pinky side toward the crowd, fingers facing the sky

Daggers

Same as Daggers but with thumb side toward the crowd, fingers facing the ground

Buckets

arms

Hands on Hips

Arms bent with hands above hips, hands in fists

Arms straight in a V position above head, hands in Buckets position. (A Low V is the opposite, with arms held down in an upside-down V.)

High V

Arms close together, straight up on either side of head, hands in Daggers

Touchdown

Punch Up

One arm straight up in a Touchdown, the other arm in Hands-on-Hips position

Diagonal

One arm in a High V, the other in a Low V, arms creating a diagonal line with Bucket fists

Arms straight out at shoulder height
with Bucket fists (You should look
like the letter T from the neck down.)

T Motion

One arm straight up in a Touchdown,
the other straight out in a T Motion

L Motion

Any arm movement described as "broken" has one or both arms bent at the elbow and held close to the body. Your hand will be shoulder height below your chin. For example, a Broken T has both arms out at shoulder height but bent at the elbow. The T is cut in half. It looks as if you're imitating a chicken!

legs

Insides of feet touch, toes point toward crowd (This is the starting point for most cheers.)

Feet Together

Lunge Front

Back leg straight, front leg bent and forward, toes pointing toward crowd

One leg straight with toes pointed toward crowd, other leg to side, bent, so knee is directly above ankle, inside of foot toward crowd

Lunge Left/Right

Balance on one straight leg with toes toward crowd, other leg is bent with foot next to and touching knee of straight leg (This position also is called "Liberty.")

Stag

The head should be up and the back straight when doing a jump.

Jumps

You've learned the basic moves and positions used in cheers. Now you're ready to learn jumps. Jumps are used in dance routines and cheers. They may feel awkward at first but will feel better with practice. Remember always to warm up and stretch before practicing jumps.

A jump is divided into three parts. The beginning of a jump is called the "prep." In the prep, your feet are together. Quickly, raise your arms into a High V and raise yourself up on your toes. Make sure your body is fully extended. Now swing your arms down in front of your body, crossing them at chest height. Bend your knees and continue swinging your arms toward a High V. Push through your legs and lift with your arms to extend your body fully. In a successful prep, this is one continuous motion.

The "lift" is phase two of a jump. At the end of the prep, your body is fully extended. Push with your legs all the way through your toes and lift yourself off the ground. Your head should be up and your back should be straight.

The "landing" is next. After you reach the highest point of your jump, bring your legs together quickly. You need to land with your feet together. Your knees should be slightly bent to absorb the impact. Try not to land flat-footed. Roll from the balls of your feet to your heels when landing. In a successful jump, a cheerleader moves continuously from one phase to the next. Fans should not see that there are three phases.

Different positions are hit in the lift phase of the jump. Here are some common positions.

The Tuck

Keeping feet together, bring your bent knees to your chest

The X

With arms in a High V and legs straight in a Low V, your knees should face the crowd (Your body will look like the letter *X*.)

With straight legs out to each side and knees facing up, your arms reach toward your toes

The Toetouch

Front leg kicks straight out with toes slightly pointed to the side, and the back leg bends with the knee facing down toward the ground

The Herkie

Same as Herkie, but back leg is to side with bent knee facing out

The Hurdler

Three cheerleaders perform a Thigh Stand. The flyer stands on the thighs of the bases.

Stunts

A "stunt" is when one or more cheerleaders are held up by the other cheerleaders. It looks like a pyramid. Doing stunts takes a lot of practice. A stunt involves people in three positions. The "base" consists of the ground people who support the flyer. The "flyer" is the person who climbs up on the base. The "spotter" watches the base and flyer to ensure safety. The spotter helps the flyer down from a stunt. Also, the spotter catches the flyer in case of a fall. All stunts can be dangerous and should never be practiced or performed without a spotter and a coach.

The Thigh Stand involves two bases and one flyer. The bases stand next to each other, facing forward. They lunge closely toward each other, hips facing forward. The feet of their bent legs are placed one in front of the other, the insides of their feet facing the crowd. The flyer stands close behind the bases. She puts one hand on each of their shoulders. She steps onto one base's "pocket," the space where the thigh and hip meet. Then she steps onto the other base's pocket. To help the flyer dismount, each base takes one of the flyer's hands with an outside arm. Then the flyer jumps down lightly.

CHAPTER FOUR

Continuing Cheerleading

Now suppose that you make your school or community cheerleading squad. You have a great season, but you want to learn more. There are a lot of other opportunities to further your cheerleading skills.

Cheerleading Camps

Attending a cheerleading camp is a good way to learn new skills and meet other cheerleaders. Most cheerleading camps are held in the summer. There are day camps and sleep-away camps. You can attend alone, with friends, or as a member of a squad.

At camp, you practice and improve your technique. You learn new cheers and chants. Many camps also teach gymnastics and advanced stunting.

Attending cheerleading camps is a good way to learn new cheerleading routines and to make friends.

At competitions, cheerleading squads compete against one another. These cheerleaders are performing at the National Cheerleading Association Championship in Dallas, Texas.

Competitions

Cheerleading is considered a sport. Cheerleading squads compete against one another in competition. There are cheerleading competitions throughout the country. The levels range from local to national competitions. One of the biggest competitions, the United Cheerleading

Association Championships, is televised on ESPN every year. Competitions at various levels—from junior high school to college—are featured. Other cheerleading organizations sponsor competitions. Contact the organizations listed in the Resources section at the back of this book for more information.

College and Professional Cheerleading

Almost every college and university with sports teams has cheerleading squads. Cheerleading is a great way to meet people on campus and to show your school spirit. Some schools even offer scholarships to cheerleaders!

Many professional football and basketball teams have cheerleading squads. These squads require dance and gymnastic skills. Some teams have more than one squad. If you are interested in trying out, you may want to study dance or take tumbling classes. That will improve your chance of making the squad.

NEW WORDS

abdominal crunch a stomach exercise similar to a sit-up

aerobic a type of exercise that improves oxygen use by the body

base the people on the ground who support the flyer during a stunt

flyer the person who climbs up on the base during a stunt

flexibility the ability to stretch, reach, and bend

megaphone a cone-shaped device used to direct and strengthen the voice

poise the ability to be calm and comfortable in front of people

NEW WORDS

pom-pom a ball of material used as a decoration and to attract attention

spotter the person who watches the base and the flyer to ensure safety during a stunt

stunt a difficult cheerleading move or trick that includes climbing, throwing, or gymnastics

synchronized performed at the same time and in the same way

FOR FURTHER READING

Books

Breaux French, Stephanie. *The Cheerleading Book: Includes Cheers, Charts, and Jumps!* Chicago, IL: Contemporary Publishing, 1995.

Kiralfy, Bob and Rob Shone, Peter Harper, Sarah Levete. *The Most Excellent Book of How to Be a Cheerleader.* Brookfield, CT: Millbrook Press, 1997.

Neil, Randy and Elaine Hart and the Staff of the International Cheerleading Foundation. *The All New Official Cheerleader's Handbook.* New York, NY: Simon and Schuster, 1986.

FOR FURTHER READING

Scott, Kieran. *Ultimate Cheerleading.*
New York, NY: Scholastic Inc., 1998.

Magazines
American Cheerleader
www.americancheerleader.com
Lifestyle Ventures LLC
250 West 57th Street, Suite 1701
New York, NY 10107

RESOURCES

Organizations
American Cheerleading Federation
www.cheeracf.com
This organization runs cheerleading camps.

Cheerleaders of America (COA)
www.coacheer.com
COA has a series of cheerleading camps and competitions for many divisions, youth through high school.

Web Sites
Cheerleading News
www.cheerleadingnews.com
This site has news and information about cheerleading and related events.

Cheer Place
www.cheerplace.com
This site offers articles and features as well as tips on cheerleading techniques.

INDEX

INDEX

About the Author

Ellen Rusconi is a former cheerleader and gymnast. She currently lives in New York City, where she works in theater on and off Broadway.